Faulty Mot

ELAINE RANDELL

Shearsman Books
Exeter

First published in the United Kingdom in 2010 by
Shearsman Books Ltd
58 Velwell Road
Exeter EX4 4LD

www.shearsman.com

ISBN 978-1-84861-089-7
First Edition

Contents

For my three daughters
Phoebe, Beatrice and Naomi

Faulty Mothering

Faulty Mothering

1991–1996

"We think back through our mothers if we are women."
Virginia Woolf

I

Slip shod
worn through all my empty threats
smarty packets   gold stars
left with maternal comfort   exhaustion
forgiveness.

Her eye saw the back of the Startrite sandal
as he turned the corner towards the pond
Don't play near the water, she said
I'm not, he shouted. Her arms pit high in
suds, legs aching. I only put my foot in
he said displaying the black silt up to his groin.
The baby woke red faced howling then stopped
suddenly. Even children who have experienced bad parenting
with no other relationships do not necessarily abuse all their
children . . .
Rachel ran in.
Is lunch ready, I'm starving.
She picked him up onto the edge of the wooden draining
board and soaked his foot in the sink,
she ran to the baby. Rachel shut up, she said and
ran past her.

II

After she was born
        they let me hold her
her soft head had slipped
from between my legs.
        Such promise.

The septicaemia put me
into the isolation ward.
I never saw her for 12 days
my milk dried
my heart stopped.
It was never the same again.

I lost what we had
        she's a stranger
                a no-one.
Outside the men were
shovelling grit into the road.
In life there is simply
no time to touch
only brush by in passing.

III

My history as a child
was torn
wanting to please
be tidy
honest faithful
and yet missing
a link a passport to the adult
world
I was muzzled   callipered
orphaned.

IV

I am tired of your trousers and shoes
she said
they are full of you.
When the twins were born
he never said 'I love you' he just said
'great' and stood up when he'd seen their
heads in the tiny plastic cots.
He never brought flowers like the other
fathers, she tried not to be hurt. She
knew he did it on purpose.
At night she would cry herself to sleep
between feeding the babies. One would
wake then the other then the other then
the other. Her breasts felt like sore bricks.
You ought to get some rest he told her.
Her friends made her go out alone but
at feeding time her milk came in and
ran down the sides of her body and formed in droplets round
        her feet.
When his family came they would love
playing with the twins, bouncing them high
and making them laugh "You are a lucky
girl," his mother said.
At dawn when the children slept she read,
"When people manage to get in touch with their own pain,
they no longer want to take it out on others".

V

There is moment inside of him that he can recall
—a crying out, arms flaying. The sides of the cot
are hard, the mattress wet, he cries out and then stops.

Damp garden clay late blue flowers   seed heads
cut down the new buds breaking through. The nights are drawing
in over our head my arms are bent double with effort. Your socks
have lost their colour in the wash.

Blackened ideas, a dream of soaring
you are there and I have lost my legs. I can never
fail to look out for you. The back of your
jumper never ceases to lift me.

The resolution to be young again to not worry
so often they seem to fade away
her tiny hand, unblemished heart. "Fish do have eyes
don't they Mummy?" she asked.

He turned on his Lotus shoe heel in the kitchen on the
Vinolay and slammed the door
"Where's Daddy going?" asked Michael.
It was the last time he ever mentioned him.

The green edge of winter has opened and into the meadow the
yellow basins of Buttercup and Vetch tangle around
the gate post.

VI

"I never asked them for much just that they kept the
wood basket topped with kindling. Then I could do
the washing on the boiler see. I had three sons
and a husband that only saw as far as his fishing line.
On the 10th November I went round the house picking
up the dirty washing, went to the Rayburn—no
kindling. They only have to do one thing, I thought,
get kindling and they can't even do that for me.

I was faced with a mud ridden kitchen, a mound
of washing no hot water and no kindling. I
found my purse put on my coat and left. I walked
up to the village and took a bus, got off and sat
down outside the church, took the bus back again
and waited till after dark and then when I could think
of nothing else to do I went home. The kitchen was
all lit up, he was making the cheese on toast,
they looked up when I came in. Then I saw the washing
still there, the fire still out, the basket empty.
No kindling. 'Where you been Mum?'
'I've been to the pictures' I said. 'Good film was
it?' he asked."

VII

The steel tempest
is a dreary shadow
I would yet half asleep.
Unnoticed the children
mittened blamed their efforts
on climate, atmosphere, money.
Paper methods.   Tawdy skin.
I will never bounce back
know the child
I am forever clipped.

VIII

We are in air
the Kent fields
cushions of harvest
ribbons of grass wind around
ankles.
His child's idea
Red as her memory
a blizzard of faces
she has found
her mother.
The old birth certificate in its folded wallet.
A sharp pain across her
eye, her back. The gate
was held closed with a dog lead.
You'd better come in,
the woman said
I remember you,
you never stopped crying.
She searched the face before her
the neck the chest,
those breasts were never for me
she knew.
She left after a
promise to meet again.
It was all in pieces again
broken up just like before.

IX

You'd better go, I told him
No use you hanging round here looking
tormented, you go and make your life
with her. He packed his clothes
into a Lo Cost carrier bag.
Can I see Leah again he asked
as he went past your bedroom
down the stairs, No I shouted
You've made your choices. I remember
he never looked back once.
I watched him from the upstairs
bedroom window. You woke up and
asked for him.
daddy will
tuck you up I said. I couldn't think
what else to say.

X

The pansies in the window box are stunning
everybody said so
I don't know where you find the time
the postman said.

In 1970 when her father died she thought she would die
too. No other balance no calm still voice to counteract
her own restless need and shrill accusations.
Twenty five years on she is older
shrill accusatory alive and calm
she has seen the red sky and pale blue trail.

She is worrying that liver they had for tea
will result in a deformity.
His palpitations may be the start of an attack
if we have another hurricane the chimney will
fall in onto the children.
The baby's head isn't growing as fast as it should
the cat's worms will result in someone losing an
eye the plant food she put on the tomatoes contained
the chemical the man on TV warned against
they are travelling on the sinking ferry
she lays her cellulite legs on the British Home Stores
polyester fitted sheet and is borne away and in the morning
is quite refreshed.

XI

At weekends
the men walk around Safeways proud
of their offspring
lay them on their backs like motorcycle parts.
In the week
the women are wrecked
look dazed with tasks
fitting life in between schooltime
jamming toddlers onto the pram tops
their legs are so heavy.

Oval is the woman's shape
her eggs are clear—honest
never scattered, permanent, stationary
internal.
Children knowing this
seek it out know here to go
for rest.

XII

The space between crying and surrender
is a handkerchief away
oblivion makes a lumpy pillow at night
contentment can only be a closing off
a kind of breaking down.

The shimmer of tears lack lustre.
In a nearby garden a young girl a mother
of a baby lay down
her head in my neighbour's Syringa, fell asleep
confused and drunk.
They took her baby inside and cleaned his little
head.
I feel sick she said.

XIII

In the prison he was in solitary
he was pleased he had explained it
all before
the psychiatrist who came drew a map
of his family, he even brought a
photograph of the child
his heart was an overblown melon
he ate the seeds, it was best.

When she became pregnant he bought her
a silver star to hang around her neck.
"I want to give you the moon" he said.
She knitted she was a picture
they all said it except her mother.
When the baby came she fed her, loved
her washed her tiny face.
A week later she threw the baby at him
"I can't do it" she said "I'm no use".
He cried, she cried, the baby cried.
The doctor came his mother arrived
the health visitor wrote things down.
"I hate you" she said to the baby.
"Lay down" they told her
The baby grew thin she became fat.
Her mother never came.
I told you I was no use she said.

XIV

The first time I shook her
I knew I would remember it
forever.
Something unchangeable had happened.
She was better in the rain
there was hope and breath.
I drank in long open
shards.
The savage lines in my heart
are forever on my face
great ditches of
poisoned forests.

XV

Or a child's face
         divine
upturned in the half light.

Ask me if I'm six
She says. Well are you?
No, I'm seven!

She moves off
content

Torment   O moon
O princess in mourning.

XVI

I can't please her ever.
I was the disappointment.
The earth is born about her
Its manners are harsh and
careless.

Once she told me I had ruined
her figure and my pig-like
eyes belonged to my father.

The rain had turned people into
fast moving, shining objects.
Its limp sculptor's
hands confirm the shape of the envy.

XVII

I looked out for her every minute
She didn't come till very late
but when she did it was funny.
Mummy didn't get out of the
car she spoke to her friends
on the CB instead. Her hands
were warm but her legs were bare
were cold. She looked away
when I said her name.

There is a breaking down
inside of her. There is a taste of
rat. It is shorn up
for good
like a dead person.

XVIII

Years later
She cannot recall the things the children said when they were tiny;
the things that made them laugh.
Like so many things, time had robbed it away leaving her naked.
Now the children are adults they say things which hurt her
Don't look like that, they say when she might cry.
Turning away towards the car park it is full of others,
all in their differing chancy stages.

XIX

And therefore was her labour much that more in washing and
        wringing

To worry
is to be connected with
The woman's lot is to worry
to be troubled with   concerned, mixed up
Loaded windless the sky takes fear, returns it laundered ready.
Waiting for fortune to happen upon them
the men take chances wonder at the reeling birds diesel streets.
more work to be done not simply tidied.

XX

The women are gathered, not in extravagant postures but huddled
    weeping, their eyes reddened and dashed.

The white daisies spring up in anticipation they are known.
Women hem garments their hands sick with action
faces wrenched with ideas and sleepless O they are sleepless
footless, heartless hurt.
wrecked reality.
Where are the men standing?
are they alone or in unison rowdy with lofty fear and rage.
Some become tearful expectant
stagger at a loss, tearful,
trounced others swagger on the bridge wide open and forgotten.
We are not simply done for there is more to understand

XXI

You could almost think, sometimes, that their mother wasn't
behind her face anymore

Nowadays the rutted furrowed steps of her brow and
Dark patches swept across like storms, sudden, a strong attack
on a defended place or position.
Bellowed beamless startled by ideas of chaos and catastrophe
There had been so many times like that   endured ridden out
Its what has to be done   a pressing on

FOR THE TIME BEING

Polaroid

Hand to head
head to hands
we shield
as if to turn inside
away from this into a better
complex
hoping to look
find ourselves
healed restored forgiven.

Unlikely the world of
human systems—body, focus pursuit
will go away
more likely it will run faster
become worse, blur
you might miss the very thing
you're doing this for.

Too busy providing
to enjoy or understand
like taking photographs of memorable things
you miss the point, out of focus
lose your turn too eager to capture.

It's a risky moment

For Evelyn

When the light breaks over the marsh
the sheep huddle together
they know what to do.
There is sometimes a coldness in man
which is borne from the timid fear
about the plight of others.
But look, the air is forgiving and
reparation and hope tug at our sleeve
it will not leave us.
At night across the marsh
the darkness is only the light waiting for its moment,
the lambs suckle quietly without us.

Animals

The vet comes out to see my sick Ram lamb that's penned up in the garage.

His long boned fingers search into the lamb's skull, searching for a cyst or growth. Bending over the body of the sick sheep he places his stethoscope against the ribs and with eyes closed and head bent as if in prayer he stays silent for a full five minutes. What's the verdict? I ask. He tells me that the Ram is suffering from a heart murmur but that isn't why he's ill. He opens the animal's mouth and presses the gum hard. The blood returns to the head quite quickly.

Eliminating worms or Staggers he suggests it could be an infection of the brain and injects the animal with fluids. Later in my kitchen he talks about life in the surgery.

He says, the farmers round here don't like us younger vets you know, they don't trust anyone that's under 60. I'm no James Herriot and I can't win them round. I tell him that I'm sure he will eventually. I hope so, he says, because I do really love animals and I like to make the quality of their short lives better.

I ask if he is married. Oh no, he says, I'm no good with girls, too awkward really. I just wish we were like animals, none of this courtship performance, just nuzzling down together and having babies.

Wouldn't Mate Again

1.
She is worrying about the limescale in the sink
the area around the taps at the back
stained and dirty.
The bleach shifts it temporarily but then it's back
again in her arms
looking up at her grinning through.
It's like him
she worries about him
whether he's bought cotton socks
for his feet, if he's drinking too much,
whether he thinks of the boy.
The boy thinks of him
calls him dad
wants him home
cries for him in sleep and names the guinea-pig Nick.

2.
Once they went fishing together
enjoyed the day he talks of it continually.
Now and again he's in a mood
walks out like his daddy swaggers
raises his hands like him
but lacks the ability thankfully
says to her, "I'm going, I hate it here,
I want to find Nick", but he returns when she's
not looking for him, finds him curled in his bed
like a baby not like a man.

3.
Next day he didn't mention it, says he's too
busy when Nick calls to say hello.
Went off on his BMX.
Nick bought
Hula Hoops and Aeros that no one ate.
She looked at the sink
worries about the limescale
looked out of the window and hoped the Guinea pigs
wouldn't mate again.

Matrimonial

She said:

He never makes decisions, it's always left to me. I ask him, he says, 'you decide'. So I do.
When it goes wrong he says, 'I told you I didn't want to do that, I said it wasn't the right time.'
But I tell him, you never said anything, not one thing.
When it goes right he says, 'I always did say that was a good idea, we should have seen to it before, if you'd listened to me we'd have been a lot better off.'
But I say, you didn't say a word, never uttered a monosyllable, not one iota of sound came from your lips. He told me my cooking was grim so then he shops for himself at Iceland and cooks it in the garage.

He said:

She's so bossy, always on about something or another.
She gets upset. I say what's wrong? Always she says 'nothing'. I tell her there must be something but usually she walks away. Later she shouts at me that I don't care about her and why don't I talk to her like other husbands. She hates cooking for me and said to do it myself. I cut the meat up with my angle grinder sometimes.

The children say:

Mummy is always in a bad mood with a cross face. She says she's tired. We draw pictures for her and she always cries and cuddles us then. Daddy's busy outside or at work, he says someone's got to look lively around here.

Once we had a very bad Christmas and daddy pulled down all the decorations and mummy burnt the dinner. Our little brother cried so much I had to take him to our next door neighbour's and blow up a balloon for him. The neighbour gave me a sip of sherry and kissed me, it wasn't very nice but I didn't tell mum, she says she's got enough on her plate.

Mummy looks happier when daddy kisses her but daddy cried when he threw the decorations away. When they didn't love each other anymore daddy said it wasn't us he was leaving but he did. Daddy lived in his car. Mummy said the car didn't need conversation, just maintaining. At the contact centre we saw daddy once and then he asked us if mummy still wanted more than he could give her. I told him she didn't make hot dinners anymore only sandwiches. Daddy cried and so we didn't see him again.

Storm Damage

The clay fields
have sunk, drowned, gone under.
The trees are limbless
amputated struck senseless.

Nature has pruned us.
Brought home our poor circulation and
dull hearts.

Concealed in our differences
our common
identities fraternities
hungers and thirsts.

We hold our palms to the wind
vulnerable and small like children
beside the adults.

Before I go or the gap left after leaving

So, what is needed?
Equipment in preparation for moving away   a logic is
needed   but,
in front of that, you need the knowledge of being loved,
known for who you are. *It's belonging* that sets the course.
A ticket and a reason to move away, to branch out or to go, to
die *to leave and to meet strangers*
so then it's a heady divide; driven, determined,
de decretar, interior, heart.

The loss within   collapse   chance *what does not*
change is the will to change
all options but   anchored, we are kept from our worst
floundering by correlation, link.
Being In mind.
The sea air is bracing
the pool charms and the plants greenery cuts with a smell   a
simple device   sensory *When the coast was not the coast and*
sea was a shell ."

So what to do before leaving
Packing away, tiding the unkempt and unravelled.
Cleaning up the spilt

When you went there was so much left behind
I hold it

For Jenny Diski

I.

With the frozen hope that keeping still will do the trick of turning back time

An atlas of your entire arm moves across a clipped face of a baby.
Listen, it was a chancy moment
On arrival, the cloud was encompassing anyway, spinning some
fandango with an aloof mystic you could never get the measure of.
So why try now?
Cut while you can before they notice
your arms being stuck out like that
so needy and wasteful, the heart like a sieve down the drain
Or is it?
Someone is catching you
Leave the arms open but don't flail
it makes a mark.

II

I reckon, not to have to do it

All that letting so much   un wheeling   free middle a   free for all
free   muddle
Permission not to cook
Taking your own slot
place divine, no end in sight. Another day a new start no alarm
no terror   need for drawn looks   survival is its own pasture
lined frock
No catastrophe waiting its turn
For once   for twice   for ever it is as it is

46

III.

For which one side could only comprehend the necessity
The other turns away

You try and there is no answer to it
Better walk on
a strategy for remaining.
Cruelty splits our sides
Battering the memory of a mothers lot.

IV.

A perfectly understandable figitness of creatures cooped up but
without any conceivable foreboding of harm

Hyper vigilant the cost is great   see how the arms flail
The looking out for   being found out
found wanting   perhaps
it's the same pricey pain
The others gawp but what do they know?
More,   *they know more than us* we shout it from the
kerbside

V

No need now to go any place at all

Arrival, it is a pact with rest.
Located
Crisis is avoided   no takers
Catastrophe lays in the margin   we leave it be ready to stalk
Calamity rests in our shoulders   the heart heaves quite primed.

SONGS FOR THE FAITHLESS

There is a moment in time when
Looking at the sky and its emptiness
We wonder about those others
who shrivelled and let go of it before us
before we did
right in front of us
and we gawped
still asked for
succour and yet
we turned
away
prats in our suits
our underclothes stained wet
hidden
not knowing what to do
where to go.
Are they there? Can they see us?
We have hope that they oversee
Mediate the worst
are they sorting things out
Are we alone
so left
cut
the quick dries.

There is a moment in time when
Watching children
We know that there is nothing to fear
No thing to worry for
since
some thing so
right
so designed means that no thing
can be
is forever tainted despite our bitter lips so easily twisted
our mouths treacherous, recreant, turned again against
so easily led
noted and seen so weak untrustworthy
We can sleep easy
Surely we could?

There is a moment in time when
chance and luck of life
spots us reeling
Opportunity splashing at our own heels so rarely
but we can harvest
we still gape at the even more luckless others
centuries of it
the wrong place
the thousands killed
not us
not yet
still lucky
a charm surely
It's simply being sensible that does it nothing more.
Spinning the dice of good health
those reckless nights and wasted days
count for little

There is a moment in time when
we shout out
seeking that father
a sanction
an end to it
It's not where you are but where you're headed
Your blossomed heart
Strung whippet heels
Flash clear slow snow

It's not when you were but when to let go
The shepherd does not loose sheep
they weather away
dissolve
their tired bones suckle earth

There is a moment in time when
The trees
The moment gives a licence we mount
spindle legs struggle but
that contact
Provides no doubt
it's more than ideas which
sway
the light
waves and duck the dawn
swoon into ashen marble
where the faithless lie
bleeding their chips are sallow
they get fat, a creasing over.

There is a moment in time when
The earth spins ahead
Seeing the coast out there rolling ahead of the marsh
The field and the dew
all to play for despite the narrowing time set into frame
pressing on our new boots.
Out there
fox hunts in the shadows
swift his velvet mouth

Songs for the Careless

Facts must be your friends, I said

Being upright was important
Staying in the middle was hardest
They watched for mistakes
The Others seem to know the tune, dancing properly to it as
        they do
She cannot get the steps right
Better instead to
leave nothing to chance
sit down don't let them see you humming the tune.
The clouds understand everything;
moving in as they do at the wrong moment changing things so
        quickly.

To see the future so drearily laid out like an allotment garden, with
each to his patch of work.

The clay soil is the most unforgiving, it holds such wetness, there
is no air.
His furrow was hardest, he trudged every boundary of her, she let
nothing in or out. Once he gave up, but then, she had left a small
part of herself behind which he brought out now and then. He
turned it in his palm over and over, the song remained settled into
his heart, he did not regret it.
The bulbs are drying out laying quietly expectant, loaded affluent.
I will take my ways and till them like soil,
raked over they will become changed, forgotten.
Friable soil is best.
In damp conditions the seeds germinate well, send their roots
down like lightening.
Life was easy for them, effortless, there was no hardship to be set
against. A pushover. She depended, leaned and inclined to his
leafy torso
but she was an add-on   an extra
an adjunct some things you just knew
she said.

Rats and rabbits die of indecision

The awkwardness of the confident; they are too sure
Persuaded, explicit they can only dream of bullets.
For them there are no dangers
Perils
Are for others
There is no risk involved nothing to look out for, avoid, all is
    welcome.
The careful won't talk, their silence watchful, shrewd
They seek help
gasp too late
already out of earshot.

Go about your business. The spur of necessity will keep you trotting about.

There's no rest, there really is no letting up the sky will swallow
        you
What we learn from this then
It's what counts.
Matters.
is remembered as the day closes down.
Notion, intention
Wit
Tolerance
All of that
His sleeves hurt
Pervasive
the deficient heaviness bruising the snake against his heart.

Leave the washing up and take a look around

Blow the report
They urged her.
She hadn't.
was it worth it?
She wouldn't know now
is it right to be always that responsible.
What had been lost
could she catch up with the dancing others
where picnics lasted
and time was not measured.
Washing up
Onus
Responsibility
Earning a wage
Being there
These
Things
Drove her
Reckless
Wasted
Welcomed.
The careless sing and bump into others
The watchful are still waiting tireless

Another night lies squandered

He saw her
Watched and noticed and spoke of it
Sought asked and spoke of it
Lay with her and spoke of it

There is blood flecked urge to go even a step further

Risk is for the secure
The non-compliant
who lean on the uncertainty of others
trading their good looks for
science
others can do the maths she said I do the business.
Along the sea line tide sucks
sucks bringing back returning clean
All laughter coughed up.

Slapdash he is thrown among the muddle. While harassed
apprentices jostle the bloody pans.

Haphazard and dissociated the walls have sunk
Nothing is where it was placed
others knew and have gone.
The sky is stripped and the dull trees stand
knowing nothing this time
no birds   blunted the victim of intensity is strewn along
the hedgerow.
The battered slices of self are fried   set apart
moved on   spat.

Is it possible to be a bit braver? Is it possible to skirt round the knowledge of your own ignorance, your half-lit fear of what might be at stake?

At night his courage wet the sheets, he struggled in dream and when wakeful worries rent his mind from his brain he thought about what might be different.
Still the edges became sharper
There was no give no kindness no knitted warmth no thing to lean upon no slack.
Risk is a loser's job   there's no certainty in giving bits of yourself away.
People sick up what they don't need.

she slept with sailors and cried when she scrubbed the floor

Knowing what's missing is half the problem she said. If you don't
     know
it's easier,
When he forgot her birthday she swallowed and made a pact
with the birds. "You won't see me cry again," she told them. They
didn't but saplings were washed away by her sorrow.
The ankle bones of her lovers were as the shells of bantam eggs;
their kisses both imagined and lost.
Out there in the sky the birds have the entire world
Under the planes and across the tree tops
there is no such thing as small moments of kindness the enormity
spans.

Strut in your scarlet coat. Put perfume behind your ear. Move across the crowded floors of the places where people met, into restaurants, with earnest look, to discuss the mathematics of the spirit, moistened with sweet white wine.

Snowdrops huddle worried to death by
Frost and silence
A man spits in the street its incendiary device
Smears the tender lips
Of the open.
In the woodland the bark nudges the grass alive

The price of comfort is death and damnation

Effortless and unstudied
they are rash by the waters edge
danger has lapped against their bleary wings
shrugged away discarded.
Being loved never leaves you, like the moon remaining.
The yearning after death affords no quiet repose or rest
which can be forgotten or tied away.

SONGS FOR THE HARMLESS

The danger is that our action maybe driven, not just by thought, but by powerful subconscious indecisions.

Was he her lightship, his Albatross, a saviour or a drain.
Was he a star to steer by or a mirage, a bud or a weed.
His fathers words in his head,
she never wanted you from the start, wanted your seed thrown
out of her, she's rubbish, crap, shite, deal with it boy.
In the street a mother is pushing her toddler who is holding a
bottle to her face, the mother is talking at a friend, the child
sobs throws the bottle to the ground.
Mayhem, chaos, chipped teeth, rape and rage, rape and rage,
buggery and stench. Salt and wound, wound and vinegar.
His mothers words and her chipped face in his head, he
controlled me, I was 15 years old, same as you now.
The muddle consumes everything
the sheets, the toys, the indecision.

His life and his death is among me all the time, it's in everything I do and who I am

Across the playing fields the swings and slide hold time
Sunken
areas where the children have passed by spent time landed on the
        swings
scuffing their feet, back and forth, back and forth. The same
        action wearing away
sunken.
Now they're adult
mature
don't come here anymore, lay low
only shoot a glance across the play area
now and again
he holds her up against the wall just there
skirt above her pants
he's an adult
trying it on.

Knives are out
It's tricky.

A dread that without his mothers eye on him, he too, would blur
and break up into pieces.

It was behind him
alright
the noise
someone creeping up
shouldn't do that to me
not from behind me
not a man.
Vomit in his face
the blade dissolved slid easily no effort
slid o so soft like a child's bottom along a bedroom floor.
The blade slipped into him without sound not like before
not like he remembered it
the gagging
the pain until he'd finished with him
leaving him there like rubbish.

Waving from the deck, your perspective is changed

As he runs he can see her face change
when she knows its him and
not his brother.
Running now the blood is in his shoes again like before
but it's not his blood today.
In the park the swings are frozen the metal chains catch at his hair.

LONG HAIR FOR BIRDS
1974

Poem: Before Breakfast I

And to never wish for you to be without this.
Morning, eyelid of the valley space and pine
beneath the knuckle of warm air /
Nothing to clamber for.
Each blade a sheath of its own home,
nature and her tidy woman strength.
Silence and vision are bright green leaves.

Poem: Before Breakfast II

You are.
Feet down in the valley mild spring
we swell into age and fruit.
A man ploughs the field, cold breath
and dry earth fly up behind.
How warm the sun is when we stand still.
River, knowing something else
runs clear quickly.

Poem: Before Dinner

What does not see is seen.
The mountains are not glass
nor is the earth ashamed of
time and its ailment.
Gulls hover to whine at juice
and promise.
Don't worry.
The air is there
very innocent and certain.

⌘

I get up to collect wood for the fire. Mike and Barry
are chopping it in the yard, swinging the axe down with
great strokes and definition, bringing the axe up again
with the log attached, down and up, finally snatches
the wood in two, grey and cream knots and grain smooth
pine. I take the wood to the fire, it glows amber and
ash, falls to the bottom keeping the new alight.

⌘

Walking down the drive to the bridge, go to the left
and along the edge of the river. I startle a Ram
who, not waiting, jumps
16 maybe 18 inches into the river, stops midway, then
paces across the stones, quick great heart beating against
the sand, races faster under a barbed fence leaving
his long hair for birds.

Lightning Source UK Ltd.
Milton Keynes UK
11 February 2010

149923UK00001B/36/P